50 Nut-Free Recipes for Safe Eating

By: Kelly Johnson

Table of Contents

- Chicken Alfredo
- Spaghetti Carbonara
- Beef Stir-Fry
- Grilled Lemon Herb Chicken
- Roasted Vegetable Salad
- Shrimp Scampi
- Baked Ziti
- Tofu Stir-Fry
- Meatballs with Marinara Sauce
- BBQ Chicken Skewers
- Veggie Quesadillas
- Pulled Pork Sandwiches
- Chicken Tenders
- Baked Sweet Potatoes
- Roasted Salmon
- Quinoa Salad with Lemon Vinaigrette
- Margherita Pizza
- Eggplant Parmesan
- Chicken Fajitas
- Pesto Pasta (without nuts)
- Beef Tacos
- Grilled Cheese Sandwich
- Shrimp Tacos
- Chicken Parmesan
- Baked Chicken with Vegetables
- Veggie Burger
- Butternut Squash Soup
- Stuffed Bell Peppers
- Egg Salad
- Caesar Salad (without nuts)
- Potato Salad
- Grilled Veggie Skewers
- Sweet and Sour Chicken
- Chicken and Rice Casserole
- Rice Pudding

- Carrot Soup
- Avocado Toast
- Pasta Primavera
- Sweet Potato Fries
- Roasted Brussels Sprouts
- Spaghetti with Garlic and Olive Oil
- Baked Fish Tacos
- Grilled Chicken Salad
- Lemon Garlic Shrimp Pasta
- Tomato Soup
- Vegetable Stir-Fry
- Chicken Fried Rice
- Mashed Potatoes
- Falafel with Tahini Sauce
- Roasted Chicken with Potatoes

Chicken Alfredo

Ingredients:

- 2 boneless chicken breasts, sliced
- 2 tablespoons olive oil
- 1/2 cup heavy cream
- 1/2 cup grated Parmesan cheese
- 1 garlic clove, minced
- 8 oz fettuccine pasta
- Salt and pepper, to taste

Instructions:

1. Cook fettuccine pasta according to package directions and set aside.
2. Heat olive oil in a skillet over medium heat. Season chicken with salt and pepper, and cook until browned and cooked through.
3. In the same skillet, add garlic and sauté until fragrant. Pour in heavy cream and bring to a simmer.
4. Stir in Parmesan cheese until melted and smooth. Add the cooked chicken and pasta to the skillet, tossing to combine.

Spaghetti Carbonara

Ingredients:

- 8 oz spaghetti
- 4 oz pancetta or bacon, diced
- 2 large eggs
- 1/2 cup grated Parmesan cheese
- 2 cloves garlic, minced
- Salt and pepper, to taste

Instructions:

1. Cook spaghetti according to package instructions. Drain, reserving 1 cup of pasta water.
2. In a skillet, cook pancetta or bacon until crispy. Add garlic and cook until fragrant.
3. In a bowl, whisk eggs and Parmesan cheese together. Add the hot pasta to the bowl, then quickly toss with the pancetta and egg mixture, adding reserved pasta water as needed to create a creamy sauce. Season with salt and pepper.

Beef Stir-Fry

Ingredients:

- 1 lb beef, thinly sliced (such as sirloin)
- 1 tablespoon soy sauce
- 2 tablespoons olive oil
- 1 red bell pepper, sliced
- 1 onion, sliced
- 1 cup broccoli florets
- 1 tablespoon ginger, minced
- 2 tablespoons oyster sauce

Instructions:

1. In a bowl, toss beef with soy sauce and set aside.
2. Heat olive oil in a pan over medium-high heat. Cook beef for 2-3 minutes until browned, then remove and set aside.
3. In the same pan, stir-fry vegetables until tender. Add ginger and oyster sauce, then return beef to the pan and toss everything together.

Grilled Lemon Herb Chicken

Ingredients:

- 4 boneless chicken breasts
- 2 tablespoons olive oil
- Juice of 1 lemon
- 2 cloves garlic, minced
- 1 tablespoon fresh thyme or rosemary
- Salt and pepper, to taste

Instructions:

1. In a bowl, combine olive oil, lemon juice, garlic, herbs, salt, and pepper.
2. Marinate chicken in the mixture for at least 30 minutes.
3. Preheat the grill to medium-high heat. Grill chicken for 5-7 minutes per side until fully cooked.

Roasted Vegetable Salad

Ingredients:

- 1 cup cherry tomatoes, halved
- 1 zucchini, sliced
- 1 bell pepper, diced
- 1 cup Brussels sprouts, halved
- 2 tablespoons olive oil
- Salt and pepper, to taste
- 4 cups mixed salad greens

Instructions:

1. Preheat oven to 400°F (200°C). Toss vegetables with olive oil, salt, and pepper. Roast for 20-25 minutes until tender.
2. Arrange roasted vegetables on a bed of salad greens and serve with your favorite dressing.

Shrimp Scampi

Ingredients:

- 1 lb shrimp, peeled and deveined
- 2 tablespoons butter
- 4 cloves garlic, minced
- 1/2 cup white wine
- 1 tablespoon lemon juice
- 8 oz spaghetti or linguine
- Fresh parsley, chopped
- Salt and pepper, to taste

Instructions:

1. Cook pasta according to package directions. Drain and set aside.
2. In a skillet, melt butter over medium heat. Add garlic and cook until fragrant. Add shrimp and cook for 2-3 minutes per side.
3. Pour in wine and lemon juice, simmer for 2 minutes. Toss pasta in the sauce, adding parsley and seasoning with salt and pepper.

Baked Ziti

Ingredients:

- 1 lb ziti pasta
- 2 cups marinara sauce
- 1 1/2 cups ricotta cheese
- 2 cups shredded mozzarella cheese
- 1/2 cup grated Parmesan cheese
- 1 tablespoon Italian seasoning

Instructions:

1. Preheat oven to 375°F (190°C). Cook ziti according to package instructions, drain.
2. In a large bowl, mix pasta with marinara sauce, ricotta, and half of the mozzarella.
3. Transfer to a baking dish, top with remaining mozzarella and Parmesan. Bake for 20-25 minutes until bubbly and golden.

Tofu Stir-Fry

Ingredients:

- 1 block firm tofu, pressed and cubed
- 2 tablespoons soy sauce
- 1 tablespoon olive oil
- 1 carrot, julienned
- 1 bell pepper, sliced
- 1 cup snap peas
- 2 tablespoons hoisin sauce

Instructions:

1. Press tofu to remove excess moisture, then cut into cubes. Toss with soy sauce.
2. Heat olive oil in a pan and cook tofu until golden on all sides, then set aside.
3. In the same pan, stir-fry vegetables for 3-4 minutes, then add tofu and hoisin sauce. Toss to combine.

Meatballs with Marinara Sauce

Ingredients:

- 1 lb ground beef or pork
- 1/4 cup breadcrumbs
- 1 egg
- 2 tablespoons parsley, chopped
- 1/2 cup grated Parmesan cheese
- 2 cups marinara sauce

Instructions:

1. Preheat oven to 375°F (190°C). Mix ground meat, breadcrumbs, egg, parsley, and Parmesan in a bowl.
2. Form mixture into meatballs and place on a baking sheet. Bake for 15-20 minutes.
3. Heat marinara sauce in a pan, add cooked meatballs, and simmer for 5 minutes. Serve with pasta or crusty bread.

BBQ Chicken Skewers

Ingredients:

- 2 boneless chicken breasts, cubed
- 1/4 cup BBQ sauce
- 1 tablespoon olive oil
- 1 teaspoon garlic powder
- 1/2 teaspoon smoked paprika
- Salt and pepper, to taste
- Skewers

Instructions:

1. Preheat the grill to medium-high heat.
2. In a bowl, mix BBQ sauce, olive oil, garlic powder, smoked paprika, salt, and pepper.
3. Thread chicken cubes onto skewers and brush with BBQ sauce mixture.
4. Grill chicken skewers for 5-7 minutes per side, until fully cooked.

Veggie Quesadillas

Ingredients:

- 2 flour tortillas
- 1/2 cup shredded cheese (cheddar, Monterey Jack, or your preference)
- 1/4 cup bell pepper, diced
- 1/4 cup onion, diced
- 1/4 cup mushrooms, sliced
- 1 tablespoon olive oil
- Salsa (optional)

Instructions:

1. Heat olive oil in a skillet over medium heat. Sauté bell pepper, onion, and mushrooms until tender, about 5 minutes.
2. Place one tortilla in a separate skillet over medium heat, sprinkle cheese on top, then add sautéed vegetables. Place the second tortilla on top.
3. Cook for 2-3 minutes per side until golden brown and crispy. Slice into wedges and serve with salsa.

Pulled Pork Sandwiches

Ingredients:

- 2 lb pork shoulder
- 1/4 cup BBQ sauce
- 1 tablespoon apple cider vinegar
- 1 teaspoon paprika
- 1 teaspoon garlic powder
- 1/2 teaspoon onion powder
- Salt and pepper, to taste
- Sandwich buns

Instructions:

1. Preheat oven to 300°F (150°C). Season pork shoulder with paprika, garlic powder, onion powder, salt, and pepper.
2. Place pork in a baking dish, cover with foil, and roast for 4-5 hours, until tender.
3. Shred pork with a fork, mix with BBQ sauce and apple cider vinegar, and serve on sandwich buns.

Chicken Tenders

Ingredients:

- 2 chicken breasts, cut into strips
- 1/2 cup flour
- 2 eggs, beaten
- 1 cup breadcrumbs
- 1 teaspoon garlic powder
- 1 teaspoon paprika
- Salt and pepper, to taste
- Oil for frying

Instructions:

1. Preheat oil in a frying pan over medium heat.
2. In three separate bowls, place flour, beaten eggs, and breadcrumbs mixed with garlic powder, paprika, salt, and pepper.
3. Dip chicken strips into flour, then egg, and coat with breadcrumbs. Fry for 3-4 minutes per side, until golden brown and crispy.

Baked Sweet Potatoes

Ingredients:

- 4 medium sweet potatoes
- Olive oil
- Salt and pepper, to taste

Instructions:

1. Preheat oven to 400°F (200°C). Pierce sweet potatoes with a fork and rub with olive oil.
2. Place on a baking sheet and bake for 40-45 minutes, until tender.
3. Serve as a side dish or top with butter, cinnamon, or your favorite toppings.

Roasted Salmon

Ingredients:

- 4 salmon fillets
- 2 tablespoons olive oil
- 1 tablespoon lemon juice
- 1 teaspoon garlic powder
- Salt and pepper, to taste
- Lemon slices, for garnish

Instructions:

1. Preheat oven to 400°F (200°C).
2. Place salmon fillets on a baking sheet, drizzle with olive oil, lemon juice, garlic powder, salt, and pepper.
3. Roast for 12-15 minutes, until salmon flakes easily with a fork. Garnish with lemon slices and serve.

Quinoa Salad with Lemon Vinaigrette

Ingredients:

- 1 cup quinoa
- 2 cups water
- 1 cucumber, diced
- 1 cup cherry tomatoes, halved
- 1/4 cup red onion, finely chopped
- 2 tablespoons olive oil
- 1 tablespoon lemon juice
- Salt and pepper, to taste

Instructions:

1. Cook quinoa according to package instructions and let cool.
2. In a large bowl, combine quinoa, cucumber, cherry tomatoes, and red onion.
3. In a small bowl, whisk together olive oil, lemon juice, salt, and pepper. Pour over the salad and toss to combine.

Margherita Pizza

Ingredients:

- 1 pizza dough (store-bought or homemade)
- 1/2 cup tomato sauce
- 1 cup fresh mozzarella, sliced
- 1/4 cup fresh basil leaves
- Olive oil, for drizzling
- Salt and pepper, to taste

Instructions:

1. Preheat oven to 475°F (245°C). Roll out pizza dough on a floured surface.
2. Spread tomato sauce over the dough, then top with mozzarella slices.
3. Bake for 10-12 minutes, until the crust is golden and cheese is bubbly.
4. Remove from the oven and top with fresh basil leaves. Drizzle with olive oil and season with salt and pepper.

Eggplant Parmesan

Ingredients:

- 2 eggplants, sliced into rounds
- 1 cup breadcrumbs
- 1/2 cup grated Parmesan cheese
- 2 cups marinara sauce
- 1 1/2 cups shredded mozzarella cheese
- 2 eggs, beaten
- Olive oil for frying

Instructions:

1. Preheat oven to 375°F (190°C). Season eggplant slices with salt and let sit for 15 minutes to draw out moisture.
2. Dip eggplant slices into egg, then coat with a mixture of breadcrumbs and Parmesan cheese.
3. Heat olive oil in a pan and fry eggplant slices until golden and crispy, about 3-4 minutes per side.
4. In a baking dish, layer fried eggplant slices, marinara sauce, and mozzarella cheese. Repeat layers and bake for 20 minutes, until bubbly and golden.

Chicken Fajitas

Ingredients:

- 2 boneless chicken breasts, sliced into thin strips
- 1 onion, sliced
- 1 bell pepper, sliced
- 1 tablespoon olive oil
- 1 tablespoon fajita seasoning
- 8 flour tortillas
- Sour cream, salsa, and guacamole (for serving)

Instructions:

1. Heat olive oil in a large skillet over medium heat.
2. Add sliced chicken, onion, and bell pepper. Sprinkle with fajita seasoning and sauté until chicken is fully cooked and vegetables are tender, about 7-10 minutes.
3. Warm tortillas in the microwave or on a skillet.
4. Serve the chicken and veggie mixture on tortillas, topped with sour cream, salsa, and guacamole.

Pesto Pasta (without nuts)

Ingredients:

- 1 lb pasta (spaghetti, penne, or your choice)
- 2 cups fresh basil leaves
- 2 cloves garlic
- 1/4 cup olive oil
- 1/4 cup Parmesan cheese, grated
- Salt and pepper, to taste

Instructions:

1. Cook pasta according to package instructions. Drain and set aside.
2. In a blender or food processor, combine basil, garlic, olive oil, and Parmesan cheese. Blend until smooth. Season with salt and pepper.
3. Toss the cooked pasta with the pesto sauce until evenly coated. Serve immediately.

Beef Tacos

Ingredients:

- 1 lb ground beef
- 1 packet taco seasoning
- 1/2 cup water
- 8 taco shells or tortillas
- Toppings: shredded lettuce, diced tomatoes, shredded cheese, sour cream, salsa, guacamole

Instructions:

1. Brown the ground beef in a skillet over medium heat, breaking it up as it cooks.
2. Drain excess fat and add taco seasoning and water. Stir and simmer for 5 minutes, until the mixture thickens.
3. Fill taco shells with the beef mixture and top with your favorite toppings.

Grilled Cheese Sandwich

Ingredients:

- 4 slices of bread
- 4 tablespoons butter
- 4 slices of cheese (cheddar, American, or your choice)

Instructions:

1. Butter one side of each bread slice.
2. Place two slices of bread, buttered side down, on a skillet over medium heat.
3. Place a slice of cheese on each piece of bread. Top with the second slice of bread, buttered side up.
4. Grill for 2-3 minutes on each side until golden brown and the cheese has melted. Serve hot.

Shrimp Tacos

Ingredients:

- 1 lb shrimp, peeled and deveined
- 1 tablespoon olive oil
- 1 teaspoon chili powder
- 1 teaspoon cumin
- 8 small tortillas
- Toppings: shredded cabbage, cilantro, lime wedges, avocado, salsa

Instructions:

1. In a bowl, toss shrimp with olive oil, chili powder, and cumin.
2. Heat a skillet over medium heat and cook the shrimp for 2-3 minutes per side until pink and cooked through.
3. Warm tortillas and assemble the tacos by placing shrimp on each tortilla, then top with cabbage, cilantro, lime, avocado, and salsa.

Chicken Parmesan

Ingredients:

- 2 boneless, skinless chicken breasts
- 1 cup breadcrumbs
- 1/2 cup grated Parmesan cheese
- 1 egg, beaten
- 1 cup marinara sauce
- 1 cup shredded mozzarella cheese
- Olive oil, for frying

Instructions:

1. Preheat oven to 375°F (190°C).
2. Mix breadcrumbs and Parmesan in a shallow dish. Dip chicken breasts into beaten egg, then coat with breadcrumb mixture.
3. Heat olive oil in a skillet and fry chicken for 4-5 minutes per side, until golden brown.
4. Place fried chicken on a baking dish, top with marinara sauce and mozzarella cheese. Bake for 20 minutes, until cheese is bubbly.

Baked Chicken with Vegetables

Ingredients:

- 4 boneless chicken breasts
- 1 tablespoon olive oil
- 1 teaspoon garlic powder
- 1 teaspoon thyme
- 1 teaspoon rosemary
- 4 cups mixed vegetables (carrots, potatoes, onions, bell peppers, etc.)
- Salt and pepper, to taste

Instructions:

1. Preheat oven to 400°F (200°C).
2. Rub chicken breasts with olive oil, garlic powder, thyme, rosemary, salt, and pepper.
3. Arrange chicken breasts and mixed vegetables on a baking sheet. Drizzle with olive oil.
4. Roast for 25-30 minutes, until chicken is cooked through and vegetables are tender.

Veggie Burger

Ingredients:

- 1 can (15 oz) black beans, drained and mashed
- 1/2 cup breadcrumbs
- 1/4 cup grated carrot
- 1/4 cup chopped onions
- 1 teaspoon garlic powder
- 1 tablespoon soy sauce
- 1 tablespoon olive oil
- 4 burger buns
- Lettuce, tomato, and your favorite condiments for serving

Instructions:

1. In a bowl, combine mashed black beans, breadcrumbs, grated carrot, onions, garlic powder, soy sauce, and olive oil. Mix until well combined.
2. Form the mixture into 4 patties.
3. Heat a skillet over medium heat and cook the patties for 4-5 minutes per side, until golden brown.
4. Serve the veggie patties on buns with lettuce, tomato, and condiments.

Butternut Squash Soup

Ingredients:

- 1 medium butternut squash, peeled, seeded, and cubed
- 1 onion, chopped
- 2 cloves garlic, minced
- 4 cups vegetable broth
- 1 tablespoon olive oil
- 1/2 teaspoon ground cinnamon
- Salt and pepper, to taste
- 1/2 cup heavy cream (optional)

Instructions:

1. Heat olive oil in a large pot over medium heat. Add onion and garlic and sauté until softened, about 5 minutes.
2. Add butternut squash, vegetable broth, cinnamon, salt, and pepper. Bring to a boil, then reduce heat and simmer for 20-25 minutes, until squash is tender.
3. Use an immersion blender or regular blender to purée the soup until smooth.
4. Stir in heavy cream if desired and adjust seasoning. Serve hot.

Stuffed Bell Peppers

Ingredients:

- 4 bell peppers, tops cut off and seeds removed
- 1 lb ground beef or turkey
- 1 cup cooked rice
- 1/2 cup chopped onions
- 1 can (15 oz) tomato sauce
- 1 teaspoon garlic powder
- 1 teaspoon dried oregano
- 1 cup shredded cheese (cheddar or mozzarella)
- Salt and pepper, to taste

Instructions:

1. Preheat oven to 375°F (190°C).
2. In a skillet, cook ground meat and onions over medium heat until browned. Add garlic powder, oregano, salt, and pepper.
3. Stir in cooked rice and tomato sauce. Simmer for 5 minutes.
4. Stuff the bell peppers with the meat and rice mixture and place them in a baking dish.
5. Top with shredded cheese and cover with foil. Bake for 30 minutes, then remove foil and bake for an additional 10 minutes until the cheese is melted and peppers are tender.

Egg Salad

Ingredients:

- 6 hard-boiled eggs, peeled and chopped
- 1/4 cup mayonnaise
- 1 tablespoon Dijon mustard
- 1 tablespoon chopped fresh dill or parsley
- 1 teaspoon lemon juice
- Salt and pepper, to taste

Instructions:

1. In a bowl, combine chopped eggs, mayonnaise, Dijon mustard, fresh dill, lemon juice, salt, and pepper.
2. Mix until well combined.
3. Serve on a bed of lettuce, as a sandwich, or with crackers.

Caesar Salad (without nuts)

Ingredients:

- 4 cups romaine lettuce, chopped
- 1/4 cup grated Parmesan cheese
- 1/2 cup croutons
- 1/4 cup Caesar dressing (store-bought or homemade)

Instructions:

1. Toss the chopped lettuce with Caesar dressing in a large bowl.
2. Add grated Parmesan cheese and croutons.
3. Toss again and serve immediately.

Potato Salad

Ingredients:

- 2 lbs potatoes, peeled and cut into cubes
- 1/2 cup mayonnaise
- 2 tablespoons Dijon mustard
- 1 tablespoon apple cider vinegar
- 2 hard-boiled eggs, chopped
- 1/2 cup chopped celery
- 1/4 cup chopped green onions
- Salt and pepper, to taste

Instructions:

1. Boil potatoes in a large pot of salted water until tender, about 10-15 minutes. Drain and cool slightly.
2. In a bowl, combine mayonnaise, mustard, vinegar, eggs, celery, green onions, salt, and pepper.
3. Add the potatoes and toss gently to combine. Chill in the refrigerator for at least an hour before serving.

Grilled Veggie Skewers

Ingredients:

- 1 zucchini, sliced into rounds
- 1 red bell pepper, cut into chunks
- 1 yellow bell pepper, cut into chunks
- 1 red onion, cut into chunks
- 1 cup cherry tomatoes
- 1 tablespoon olive oil
- 1 teaspoon dried oregano
- Salt and pepper, to taste

Instructions:

1. Preheat the grill to medium-high heat.
2. Thread the vegetables onto skewers, alternating between zucchini, bell peppers, onion, and tomatoes.
3. Brush the skewers with olive oil and sprinkle with oregano, salt, and pepper.
4. Grill for 6-8 minutes, turning occasionally, until vegetables are tender and slightly charred.

Sweet and Sour Chicken

Ingredients:

- 1 lb chicken breast, cut into bite-sized pieces
- 1/4 cup cornstarch
- 2 tablespoons vegetable oil
- 1/2 cup pineapple chunks
- 1/2 cup bell pepper, diced
- 1/4 cup onion, diced
- 1/4 cup sugar
- 1/4 cup vinegar
- 2 tablespoons ketchup
- 1 tablespoon soy sauce

Instructions:

1. Toss chicken pieces in cornstarch to coat.
2. Heat vegetable oil in a skillet over medium heat and cook chicken until golden and crispy. Remove and set aside.
3. In the same skillet, sauté bell pepper and onion for 2-3 minutes.
4. Add sugar, vinegar, ketchup, soy sauce, and pineapple chunks to the skillet. Stir and cook for 5 minutes, until the sauce thickens.
5. Return the chicken to the skillet and toss to coat in the sauce. Serve hot.

Chicken and Rice Casserole

Ingredients:

- 2 cups cooked chicken, shredded
- 2 cups cooked rice
- 1 can (10.5 oz) cream of mushroom soup
- 1/2 cup sour cream
- 1 cup shredded cheddar cheese
- 1/2 cup frozen peas
- Salt and pepper, to taste

Instructions:

1. Preheat oven to 375°F (190°C).
2. In a large bowl, combine chicken, rice, cream of mushroom soup, sour cream, peas, salt, and pepper.
3. Transfer the mixture to a greased baking dish and top with shredded cheese.
4. Bake for 25-30 minutes, until the cheese is melted and bubbly.

Rice Pudding

Ingredients:

- 1/2 cup white rice
- 4 cups milk
- 1/2 cup sugar
- 1/2 teaspoon vanilla extract
- 1/2 teaspoon ground cinnamon (optional)

Instructions:

1. In a saucepan, bring 2 cups of water to a boil. Add rice and cook for 15-20 minutes until tender.
2. Stir in milk, sugar, and vanilla extract. Cook over medium heat for 20-25 minutes, stirring occasionally, until the pudding thickens.
3. Remove from heat and cool slightly. Sprinkle with cinnamon if desired. Serve warm or chilled.

Carrot Soup

Ingredients:

- 4 cups carrots, peeled and chopped
- 1 onion, chopped
- 2 cloves garlic, minced
- 4 cups vegetable broth
- 1 teaspoon ground ginger
- 1/4 cup heavy cream (optional)
- Salt and pepper, to taste

Instructions:

1. In a large pot, sauté onion and garlic in olive oil until softened.
2. Add carrots, vegetable broth, and ground ginger. Bring to a boil, then reduce heat and simmer for 25-30 minutes until carrots are tender.
3. Use an immersion blender to purée the soup until smooth. Stir in heavy cream if desired. Season with salt and pepper. Serve warm.

Avocado Toast

Ingredients:

- 2 slices of bread, toasted
- 1 ripe avocado
- 1 tablespoon lemon juice
- Salt and pepper, to taste
- Red pepper flakes (optional)

Instructions:

1. Mash the avocado with lemon juice, salt, and pepper in a bowl.
2. Spread the mashed avocado evenly on the toasted bread.
3. Top with red pepper flakes for extra flavor, if desired. Serve immediately.

Pasta Primavera

Ingredients:

- 12 oz pasta (penne or spaghetti)
- 1 tablespoon olive oil
- 1 cup broccoli florets
- 1 red bell pepper, sliced
- 1 zucchini, sliced
- 1/2 cup cherry tomatoes, halved
- 2 cloves garlic, minced
- 1/4 cup grated Parmesan cheese
- Salt and pepper, to taste

Instructions:

1. Cook pasta according to package instructions. Drain and set aside.
2. In a large skillet, heat olive oil over medium heat. Add broccoli, bell pepper, zucchini, and garlic. Sauté for 5-7 minutes until vegetables are tender.
3. Add the cooked pasta to the skillet and toss with vegetables.
4. Stir in Parmesan cheese and season with salt and pepper. Serve warm.

Sweet Potato Fries

Ingredients:

- 2 large sweet potatoes, peeled and cut into fries
- 2 tablespoons olive oil
- 1 teaspoon paprika
- 1/2 teaspoon garlic powder
- Salt and pepper, to taste

Instructions:

1. Preheat oven to 400°F (200°C).
2. Toss sweet potato fries with olive oil, paprika, garlic powder, salt, and pepper.
3. Spread fries in a single layer on a baking sheet.
4. Bake for 25-30 minutes, flipping halfway, until crispy and golden. Serve immediately.

Roasted Brussels Sprouts

Ingredients:

- 1 lb Brussels sprouts, trimmed and halved
- 2 tablespoons olive oil
- 1 teaspoon garlic powder
- Salt and pepper, to taste

Instructions:

1. Preheat oven to 400°F (200°C).
2. Toss Brussels sprouts with olive oil, garlic powder, salt, and pepper.
3. Spread on a baking sheet and roast for 20-25 minutes, stirring halfway through, until crispy and golden brown. Serve hot.

Spaghetti with Garlic and Olive Oil

Ingredients:

- 12 oz spaghetti
- 1/4 cup olive oil
- 4 cloves garlic, thinly sliced
- 1/4 teaspoon red pepper flakes (optional)
- Fresh parsley, chopped (for garnish)
- Salt, to taste

Instructions:

1. Cook spaghetti according to package instructions. Drain, reserving 1/2 cup pasta water.
2. In a large skillet, heat olive oil over medium heat. Add garlic and red pepper flakes, cooking until fragrant, about 1-2 minutes.
3. Add the cooked pasta to the skillet, tossing to coat. If needed, add reserved pasta water to reach desired consistency.
4. Season with salt and garnish with fresh parsley. Serve immediately.

Baked Fish Tacos

Ingredients:

- 1 lb white fish fillets (such as tilapia or cod)
- 1 tablespoon olive oil
- 1 teaspoon chili powder
- 1/2 teaspoon cumin
- 1/2 teaspoon paprika
- Salt and pepper, to taste
- 8 small corn tortillas
- 1/2 cup shredded cabbage
- 1/4 cup salsa
- 1/4 cup sour cream
- Lime wedges (for serving)

Instructions:

1. Preheat oven to 375°F (190°C).
2. Rub fish fillets with olive oil, chili powder, cumin, paprika, salt, and pepper.
3. Place fish on a baking sheet and bake for 12-15 minutes, until cooked through and flaky.
4. Warm tortillas in a dry skillet or oven.
5. Flake the fish and assemble tacos with shredded cabbage, salsa, sour cream, and a squeeze of lime. Serve immediately.

Grilled Chicken Salad

Ingredients:

- 2 chicken breasts
- 1 tablespoon olive oil
- 1 teaspoon dried oregano
- Salt and pepper, to taste
- 4 cups mixed salad greens
- 1/2 cucumber, sliced
- 1/2 red onion, thinly sliced
- 1/2 cup cherry tomatoes, halved
- 1/4 cup balsamic vinaigrette

Instructions:

1. Preheat grill to medium-high heat.
2. Rub chicken breasts with olive oil, oregano, salt, and pepper.
3. Grill chicken for 6-7 minutes per side, until cooked through. Let rest for 5 minutes before slicing.
4. Toss salad greens, cucumber, red onion, and cherry tomatoes in a large bowl.
5. Top with grilled chicken slices and drizzle with balsamic vinaigrette. Serve immediately.

Lemon Garlic Shrimp Pasta

Ingredients:

- 8 oz spaghetti or linguine
- 1 lb shrimp, peeled and deveined
- 3 tablespoons olive oil
- 4 cloves garlic, minced
- 1/4 teaspoon red pepper flakes
- Juice of 1 lemon
- 1/4 cup chopped fresh parsley
- Salt and pepper, to taste

Instructions:

1. Cook pasta according to package instructions. Drain, reserving 1/2 cup pasta water.
2. In a large skillet, heat olive oil over medium heat. Add garlic and red pepper flakes, cooking for 1-2 minutes until fragrant.
3. Add shrimp to the skillet and cook for 3-4 minutes until pink and cooked through.
4. Add cooked pasta, lemon juice, and parsley to the skillet. Toss everything together, adding reserved pasta water if needed. Season with salt and pepper. Serve immediately.

Tomato Soup

Ingredients:

- 1 tablespoon olive oil
- 1 onion, chopped
- 2 cloves garlic, minced
- 2 cans (15 oz) crushed tomatoes
- 2 cups vegetable broth
- 1 teaspoon dried basil
- 1/2 teaspoon sugar
- Salt and pepper, to taste
- 1/4 cup heavy cream (optional)

Instructions:

1. Heat olive oil in a large pot over medium heat. Add onion and garlic, cooking until softened, about 5 minutes.
2. Stir in crushed tomatoes, vegetable broth, basil, and sugar. Bring to a simmer and cook for 15 minutes.
3. Use an immersion blender to purée the soup until smooth. Season with salt and pepper.
4. Stir in heavy cream if desired. Serve warm.

Vegetable Stir-Fry

Ingredients:

- 2 tablespoons vegetable oil
- 1 bell pepper, sliced
- 1 zucchini, sliced
- 1 carrot, julienned
- 1 cup broccoli florets
- 2 tablespoons soy sauce
- 1 tablespoon hoisin sauce
- 1 teaspoon sesame oil
- 1 tablespoon rice vinegar
- Cooked rice (for serving)

Instructions:

1. Heat vegetable oil in a large skillet or wok over medium-high heat.
2. Add bell pepper, zucchini, carrot, and broccoli, and stir-fry for 5-7 minutes until tender-crisp.
3. Stir in soy sauce, hoisin sauce, sesame oil, and rice vinegar. Cook for an additional 2 minutes.
4. Serve the stir-fry over cooked rice. Serve hot.

Chicken Fried Rice

Ingredients:

- 2 cups cooked rice (preferably cold)
- 2 tablespoons vegetable oil
- 2 chicken breasts, diced
- 1/2 cup frozen peas and carrots
- 2 cloves garlic, minced
- 2 eggs, beaten
- 3 tablespoons soy sauce
- 1 tablespoon sesame oil
- 2 green onions, chopped

Instructions:

1. Heat vegetable oil in a large skillet or wok over medium-high heat. Add diced chicken and cook until browned and cooked through. Remove chicken and set aside.
2. In the same skillet, add garlic and frozen peas and carrots. Cook for 3-4 minutes.
3. Push the vegetables to one side and pour beaten eggs into the skillet. Scramble until cooked through.
4. Add cold rice, cooked chicken, soy sauce, and sesame oil. Stir to combine and cook for 5 minutes.
5. Top with chopped green onions and serve immediately.

Mashed Potatoes

Ingredients:

- 2 lbs potatoes (Yukon Gold or Russet)
- 1/2 cup milk
- 1/4 cup butter
- Salt and pepper, to taste
- 2 cloves garlic, minced (optional)

Instructions:

1. Peel and cut potatoes into chunks. Place in a large pot and cover with cold water.
2. Bring to a boil and cook for 15-20 minutes until potatoes are tender when pierced with a fork.
3. Drain the potatoes and return them to the pot. Add butter and mash until smooth.
4. Heat milk in a small saucepan or microwave until warm, then slowly add to the mashed potatoes.
5. Stir in garlic, salt, and pepper to taste. Serve warm.

Falafel with Tahini Sauce

Ingredients:

For the Falafel:

- 1 1/2 cups dried chickpeas (soaked overnight)
- 1 onion, chopped
- 1 cup fresh parsley
- 1/2 cup fresh cilantro
- 4 cloves garlic, minced
- 1 teaspoon cumin
- 1 teaspoon coriander
- Salt and pepper, to taste
- 1/2 teaspoon baking soda
- 1-2 tablespoons flour (if needed)
- Vegetable oil for frying

For the Tahini Sauce:

- 1/4 cup tahini
- 2 tablespoons lemon juice
- 1 tablespoon olive oil
- 1 garlic clove, minced
- 2-3 tablespoons warm water
- Salt to taste

Instructions:

For the Falafel:

1. In a food processor, combine chickpeas, onion, parsley, cilantro, garlic, cumin, coriander, salt, and pepper. Pulse until the mixture is coarse but holds together when pressed.
2. Add baking soda and 1 tablespoon of flour, then pulse again. If the mixture is too wet, add a little more flour.
3. Cover and refrigerate for at least 1 hour.
4. Shape the mixture into small balls or patties, about 1 1/2 inches in diameter.
5. Heat vegetable oil in a deep pan over medium-high heat. Fry the falafel in batches until golden brown and crispy, about 4-5 minutes per side.
6. Drain on paper towels.

For the Tahini Sauce:

1. In a bowl, combine tahini, lemon juice, olive oil, garlic, and a pinch of salt.
2. Gradually add warm water until the sauce reaches a smooth, pourable consistency.
3. Serve falafel warm with tahini sauce on the side.

Roasted Chicken with Potatoes

Ingredients:

- 1 whole chicken (about 3-4 lbs)
- 4 large potatoes, peeled and cut into chunks
- 2 tablespoons olive oil
- 1 tablespoon dried rosemary
- 1 tablespoon thyme
- 1 lemon, quartered
- 4 garlic cloves, smashed
- Salt and pepper, to taste

Instructions:

1. Preheat oven to 425°F (220°C).
2. Place the chicken in a roasting pan. Stuff the chicken cavity with lemon wedges and garlic cloves. Drizzle with olive oil and season with rosemary, thyme, salt, and pepper.
3. Arrange the potato chunks around the chicken in the roasting pan. Drizzle the potatoes with olive oil and season with salt, pepper, and rosemary.

4. Roast for 1 hour 15 minutes, or until the chicken reaches an internal temperature of 165°F (75°C) and the potatoes are golden and tender.
5. Let the chicken rest for 10 minutes before carving. Serve with roasted potatoes.

www.ingramcontent.com/pod-product-compliance
Lightning Source LLC
LaVergne TN
LVHW061950070526
838199LV00060B/4068